DREAM

OF

NO ONE

BUT

MYSELF

Dream of No One but Myself

David Bradford

Brick Books

Library and Archives Canada Cataloguing in Publication
Title: Dream of no one but myself / David Bradford.
Names: Bradford, David (Poet), author.
Description: Poems.
Identifiers: Canadiana (print) 20210225149 |
Canadiana (ebook) 2021022519X | ISBN 9781771315609
(softcover) | ISBN 9781771315616 (HTML) |
ISBN 9781771315623 (PDF)
Classification: LCC PS8603.R3285 D74 2021 | DDC C811/.6—dc23

Fourth printing, January 2023

We acknowledge the Canada Council for the Arts, the Government of Canada through the Canada Book Fund, and the Ontario Arts Council for their support of our publishing program.

Canada | Canada Council for the Arts | Conseil des arts du Canada | ONTARIO ARTS COUNCIL CONSEIL DES ARTS DE L'ONTARIO an Ontario government agency un organisme du gouvernement de l'Ontario

The author photo was taken by Sarah Bodri.
The book is set in Thorndale (Monotype Studio) and Inter (Rasmus Andersson).
Designed by LOKI.
Printed and bound by Coach House Printing.

BRICK BOOKS

487 King St. W.
Kingston, ON K7L 2X7
www.brickbooks.ca

Though much of the work of Brick Books takes place on the ancestral lands of the Anishinaabeg, Haudenosaunee, Huron-Wendat, and Mississaugas of the Credit peoples, our editors, authors, and readers from many backgrounds are situated from coast to coast to coast in Canada on the traditional and unceded territories of over six hundred nations who have cared for Turtle Island from time immemorial. While living and working on these lands, we are committed to hearing and returning the rightful imaginative space to the poetries, songs, and stories that have been untold, under-told, wrongly told, and suppressed through colonization.

Table of Contents

We must always consider the bigger
book of grief.

—Dawn Lundy Martin

I waited for it to dry. I waited. I waited
for it to dry, then I stopped waiting.

—Renee Gladman

and she keeps saying   it's
all this time been her mother's

As in venting or vein   an acorn
less for corning   an in vain

or cornered bowing   per a
corned beef   a wind

for dehorning steers

She's said it again and again

and now I hear it
by myself down Palmerston

She's said an acorned biffing
I hear it blow down Euclid

a vent by corn and hoofing
by Laundry up Clinton

by gust and howling
to keep pace with

Ma petite cocotte   she'd call me

My petite cup of tannins
pitting the storm drains

My personal fruit
for another shorter day

That cool air and squashing boredom of the basement. July through the Masonite door. Down off the den past the laundry room. And its second toilet running. Past the four-foot darkness of the looming crawl space. And behind the office door. His pounding fingers on the keyboard. The smell of another of his Navy Cuts filling the open. Summer makeovers on Oprah on his old TV in the background. And blaring across the doors on the Trinitron. I make my Oprah louder. Clapping back through the walls. To lure him out again. Hot curly fries and Velveeta plates. I turn the oven on. Swimming in his sweatshirt. Blood around the hem. Scraping across my skinned shins. Cleaned clear off in the backyard. In my little pool. Shaped like a turtle. I jousted a boy on a bicycle. And now reach for the timer on the dash. Wobbling the footstool. Creaking as the shirt catches. On a knob. Clicking on. The orange light. She always told him. Her long way home from work. To watch for. Getting dinner going. A good boy. Gets shit done.[1]

1 A while into university, the first time around. I take little nail scissors to the one pox on my belly. And sheer out a perfect little pearl. Then sheer out the next one. Thirty times or so. Nothing I can't cut off.

And then I put it in a story for workshop. My stories about the things I go to. That make me look bad. To better bear myself.

Somehow, that same year, a few stairs above him in the staircase to the den while home on a lunch break, I said, *You know, you don't have to be angry*, reaching for his face. Somehow expecting him to open up this way. Which prompted him to throw me at the living room loveseat. And for me to just give up on him. Maybe I'd destroy him instead. That secret bit. Not once considering how condescending all of it might have felt.[2]

2 This man who cried at *The Cider House Rules*. And *Hook*. The crook in his voice. Someplace else. And tried to take my taped copy of *Pete's Dragon* when he left.

like patched-up drywall
New hope in wallpapering
True love yellows lousy with flowers

Then that bratty medley of
pink moon and purple rain
Deep water over latex Good old neon
Old smartass 2 oz. pac blood All
those second thoughts Pastel blues
minding winter like street salt

Then blessed rancid golden-hour greens
Shade and leaves like frosted tips
Illest accents Way before this

Brushed over salt peanuts
and rank citizens Zink oxide
Antique blacks all up in whites
right up to the little edges

Fleshed out long talks
in all them good voices

and ain't no one scares

Out and Out

Just I woke up

the vision of a wet spot

drowned in
how much good
there was to go on

just knowing bodies
can be the easier parts or

your latest clammy garden's

slick moonlight oil only I could
breadstick breadstick breadstick

Hankering

dreamy beeswax lips
slowly proffering

your dream bleeding
below your dream belt

pulsing our rain song
cherry lip balm breaths
pooling in my hand

pearling in
each palmed line struck in
come to mind
and out and out

clean as salt water
to my bleeding gums
pink and ginger cake
your sweetheart milk

Like there's not much minding
this yeast infection
on your period

or my failures

all this breaking
like bread

Like   that I had stopped
eating myself and
ate what yourself can't take
glad to take it

like so much
material   welcome
so much good started
no breathing

this grown trickle   lapping
where I need   needed
a wave

like when it breaks
but doesn't break

then again
new as ancient

is coming.

Just like last night.

And now you tell me
to roll when I pack?

And these are your panties?

Do they look nice?

My girlfriend's shower is a perfectly reasonable place to cry a little bit at the thought of my mother dying, hypothetically, without warning. Warmer than warm, it's private, dim, dirty-window lit, and with plenty of tea tree oil products for a complementary burning.

The death of a parent, especially a last-remaining parent, is where siblings come in handy, I think: in at least knowing that, somewhere out there, in the alabaster country of an Eastern Township or the yesteryear plantations of Pennsylvania, there is another person, who may understand very little about you, piecing together some of the same grief. When I cry in the shower, though, I'm an only child, only grandchild, a single-parent project. And all the pieces are mine.

The way I imagine it, I hear it mid-conversation. Something about so-and-so's concept of radical indistinctness, or so-and-so's catalyzing "weak" grammar, or discussing so-and-so's poem hidden within an ancient boating lecture. Something unabashed and embarrassing about so-and-so's essayistic joy and manic lows. I imagine myself saying, *Well, it's interesting that you should say that*, all undue faith in the moment, when, I imagine, my phone rings. No idea who's on the other end. Then the announcement in tiny, simple, flat sentences there's no repeating. My pathologically stable, reliable, good-with-savings, rock-ish and lifelining, French-Canadian, five-foot-tall, better-than-yours mom dispatched via the unanticipated and immediate. An accident. My mother, who never lost a point off her driver's license, thrown from the car impressively. Surrounded by a slow flurry of police wondering about the coffee. A dead body, which can wait. And back in the shower, I imagine the news makes me cry. And I imagine it perfectly because I'm crying.

I'm crying because I'm turning over how much of me she's made possible, and wondering how much of what is decent in me is hers. Not just in light of how awful I once was (and the awful ways we can all behave toward our mothers), but how little I may have felt a need to struggle out of that awfulness if it wasn't for her example. The good handwringing she won't admit, if pressed, is her doing. How what I've managed is, maybe, the creative, temperamental iteration of the way she can't help but live. How much of that may falter once she's departed. How I might long for her haunting. How I might long for the reading she's yet to give me.[3] The shower grows colder with every second.

I think, *Call your mother, call your mother*, before I forget.

What if my mother dies slowly, slowly lost to herself, too, as I lose her along the way?

3 I just want her to read me. The little asshole who wants her caught up to what I like. He's thinking she might enjoy this Margaret Christakos. He's thinking book of essays, sort of, on matriarchs, aging mothers, more or less. Pigeonholing her. A gateway book, perhaps.

When I try to feel it out on the phone, she tells me she's been reading about five books a week. Mostly about condos, and finance. Learning everything she can.

So we talk about that instead.

whose child combed

way

The nowhere headed

from

Who heard

start

to pay for it

a

Gab better

Dragging on bargain

freckled

hook-nose *Whose* I own

The Plot

Won't let your bad self.
Let go of your old debt.

Tiring of your old self.
Won't let your made bed.

Let your bad blood let.
Your grown debt get.

That grown self to sleep.

The what the fuck I meant.
In that slump long wind

clapping. Spitting storm
mean out my slow will. Head

a drum out the old lived.
Home won't my slow chill.

Say goodbye to me.
Or ghost off in the burning.

A markedly austere sulf les t... tent, the
2014 ... odynamic, the fizz of CO2 airing
o... presents a bold blood-clot violet, cocoa
and ... red meaty on the nose, clove and
... too-ripe citrus and ...
st... robust tannins, ... b...
and (if you'll just hear me out), as a go...
friend of our winemaker once ventured, a
hint, just a faint, faint trace of a savory
rustic pulse to its oaky but playful ...
something dark but silly. S...
South Central clowning gone ...
its acidic, raw-milk sting. Like the alkaline
zing of a hand buzzer? ... just a lash of
greasy rubber chicken and ... mid-tongue?
The funky, salt-chocolate ... of dance-off
and talcum. And the matching floppy shoe
bunion sweat, ... on fat cajoled in a musky
fo... dewy, peckerwood
brett, ... like skids, a kind of
decaying ... us filth, which can't help
but evoke sla... tar pit flesh. Pagliacci
... grime and blood-soaked ... the
full-bodied, ... an old scythe or
hacksaw ... gunpowder, rocksalt)
owning the ... ancing the
middle passage between ...
harvest. The ... after ... Syrah,
Viognier and Grenache ... and
cow in the valley breeze year round. A
quartzy crispness, having heard and seen
everything, ... night in ... fruit ...
Almost ... a table wine.

A ... bites content,
the ... (all ... day ... the fizz of CO2
aiming ...) pistachio ... blood-clot
cocoa and cured meat on the nose,
and currant ... citrus and allspice, but
still-robust tan ... bramble, bite,
... (if ... out), as a good
...
something ... silly. Something of
South Central clowning gone ol' country
its acidic, raw-milk ... Like it
... and blazer. Like
... chicken and ha...
... salt-chocolate BO ... dance-off
and talc ... and the m...
bunion ... bacon ... a musky
forest floor earthiness ... peckerwood
brett, smoky ... a kind of
decaying coniferous ... which I can't help
but evoke slaughter ... flesh. Pagliacci
lacrime and blood ... rainbow wigs, the
full-bodied, acrid ... of an old sc... he or
... (ever ... rock salt)
... dancing
the ... passed ... between our words
and ... harvest ... ringing ...
... Syrah, Viognier and Grenache
... ting spruce and ... in the valley
yeah round ... A ... crazy ... crisanes
heard and seen in everything ... right in
but fruity ... just candied, for ... able wine.

Cause the minute I burned it.
We were together again.

Palm pleated in the pomade.
All blue magic guarantee

of our broke-ass small pack wave.
Already too dark to see and.

That indigo shimmer shade and.

Already our old bloodied teeth.
Our old flesh in a braid.

woke
now
all
income
myself,
out
how

Singing my angry maybe
dad's bad pentameter way.

How I get so carsick I grieve.
Brown-bag the lowing heat.

The whole palpable Philly rides
all the way to the service.

His old value human gift.
Dust in a pine can. Six

years in the Delaware
I ain't ever getting back. No

plot. Ever safe from anyone.
Too late to help. Or stop

letting what I lost.
Be what I lost.

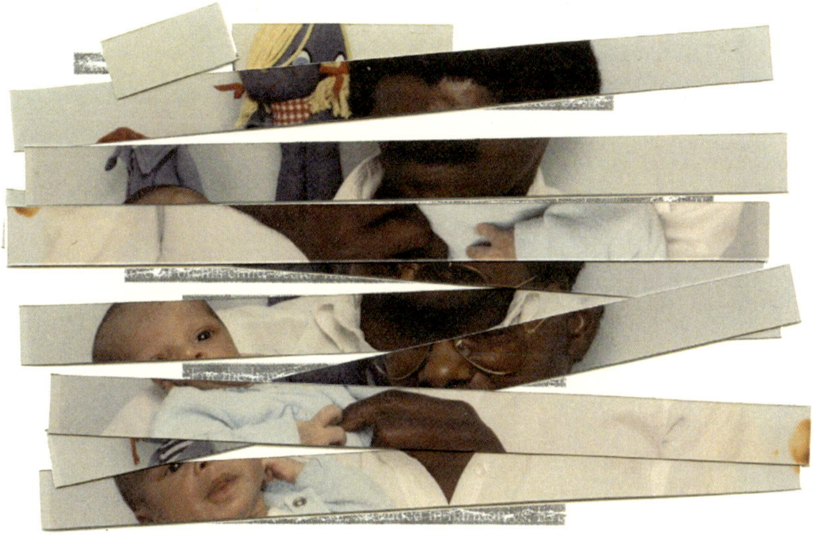

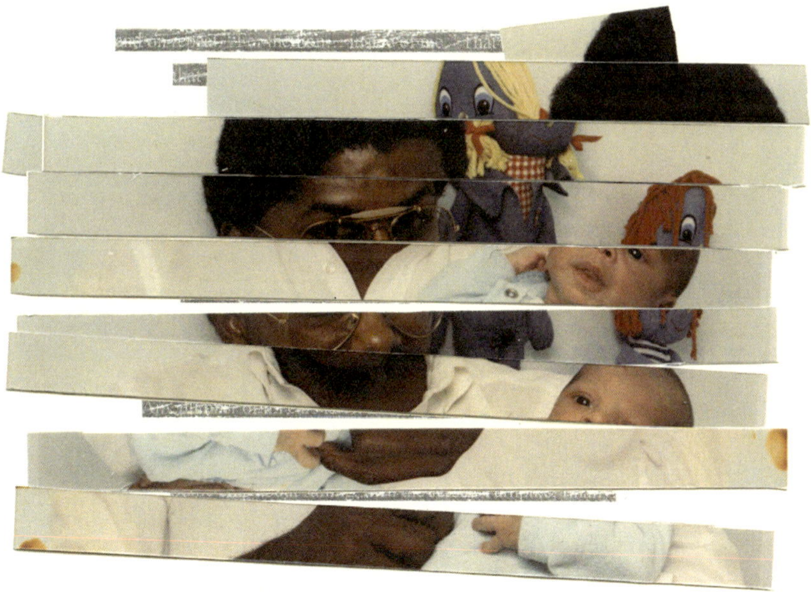

Twenty-three years after the **fact**, I wonder why **the bat** is what I got out. Why, **knowing** the seemingly unavoidable need to get something out, I decided that something was **the bat**. My mother's **arms** in my father's hands clamped to the west-facing wall of the kitchen. The word *woman* bouncing about before lunch. Not new but worse. **The bat** out of the **toy** trunk.

But what was the **argument** about? Money, I think.[4] **Or**, maybe **more likely**, me, the son trying **to turn** everyone against him? Something that became **truer** the more I heard it **repeated**.

I couldn't say for sure, and I'm not sure my mother could either. How small she **look**ed—almost **off her** feet, totally, mechanically pinned. His coffee **breath** sweeping across her face. And me, about ten, **inching down** the staircase, my size-27 aluminum in hand—*Flite* in an italic glide, **a** dynamo sky-blue swing, its **cursive length**—crying.

At least I think I was crying.[5] Not at the thought of him getting hurt, but of her or me getting hurt. **Or what** necessity looked like for a minute. How even **holding** a bat, a father **remains** enormous. How I remained **a** child. And **fear** of getting hurt, and of maybe killing him. But happy to go for his not **moving**. But somehow paralyzed, convinced regret would be triggered by death—his. **Or** what if he had made me **a** permanently **dark little** thing? The fear that she could see it. That he **didn't**.[6]

4 Where was I watching from? Before she went into the house. Just as it started up.

5 I recall: him on the front porch, in a premium cotton Barbarian rugby shirt and pleated 501s. Hi-Tec hikers, mid-holler. About brunch and shopping. Or open houses way out by the golf course. Through the ugly entryway circle thing—the 14 years it would take her to save toward ridding the house of it.

The front door, I think, wide open. Me flanking it from the inside? A little hidden? Crying?

6 The way she barely frowned at how to get him back in the house in a minute. Pretending to not consult the real budget he would never be consulted on. Which he had agreed to. Even insisted on. And resented her for it.

So, willing to use the bat but horrified of what it might mean. Were it just a threat. *Don't make me use this; I want to use this; you don't want me to use this.*[7] Something from my mother's own father-bound threats. Telling her father, as a teenager, what would happen if he slapped her again, which is how it ended—a story I was raised on. And then, though I don't think I had knowingly metabolized it, there the story was, repeating itself. Past the eye-roll that must have met her umpteenth retelling—my own necessary version of her moment. My father, his poor choices, her straining stuckness. And his son, whom he wouldn't have on his Little League team till she begged him into agreeing to it, now on the other side of the table with a triple-hitting bat. And stopping him.[8]

7 Her face still weathering the exhaustion from the last money argument. As seen from under the basketball hoop in the driveway? The haze of her next migraine? Still four years out from divorce.

8 Not a new piece of clothing on her in three years. Her white PVC Woolco soles stained a permanent turtle green from mowing the lawn. The back of her hand on her face, wiping what sweat it can.

My nose running with mulch. My feet in the grass? Couldn't mow it myself. A relief at the time. Trailing her back in the house from the door on the side?

She doesn't remember any of it. Not that time. Like it all happened to someone else.

The way I remember my mother's mother
best is licking butter off a spoon
in her muumuu by stovetop light.

Her AM radio chattering off her left wrist.

My uncle in his forties at the other end
of the apartment, watching YTV. Quiet.
My own big spoon in hand.

A few minutes before bed and:
granny elephant and baby elephant
visit her sisters in Sherbrooke;

granny tigress and baby tiger take
the Greyhound to the Granby Zoo.
Rhino fam-jams at the Biodôme.

And sleeping head to foot.

The year we spent that way before kindergarten. No money for daycare while my mother covered his tuition.

Jeff's Pretty Meh about That Shit Being Racist

Again   palms up
real coins and blue blood   Now
    no   I'll repeat it
            He says
                    I don't
care about your
    fucking change you
        didn't pay for your

      slice   you
                    An [bates breath]

            -word not there
                like an   -word
                    whistle

The pecorino ATM
    the cook watched over
      too poor   a witness

[...]   Like an grana sausage bell

Like tight cut-offs
      bufala chamois
    fontina acetate
        tortoise   shit
                    still
too middle brackish to
      play off this [hands up
    and down this penny-bun skin] still
        grainy as whole wheat

My [sighs]

first fucking time
in here and you
give me this shit

[...]

Maybe you
shouldn't come
in here then

Exactly what he said

Which sat so fine [sucks teeth]
with the roommate's lentils parmesan

I almost apologize for telling him

I almost apologized for telling him

Nobody's Sleeping

Poor man retirement still
    the old sorghum thwacker
round his pile of butts never gone

and the landlord's lungs still
    halfway to drowned
on the porch lawn chair at 2am

    Our wee widowers still
        spot-checking brunswick
for young blood and dead skin

        Our four-bypass lord still
    village king of the carton
            and not dying

the better to shut down
whatever's not his love
    for his departed marta

        I can always smell
                    smoking

    So for now home means
knowing you can't ever
        be here to listen in

    to how far this is
from you melting
        down on me

        like the softer
            of our softies

in the theatre district

Remember that day?
Then our mouths numb
working lemon water easy

Now the month and six
hours in between lifelines
a white noise machine

and so sleepy

Our dick and slit gifs
just so tiny

And your voice is cracking

And how drunk
is a drink?

What did you say?

What

What did you say?

Why Can't We Live Together

Here's how white a street can be lit A cozy close
circuit And still look like a fuckboi everywhere.

Even garage doors are all up in it like HIGHER
D2F CHILL and I'm like closing my eyes

for a minute Consent Not To Be A Single Being
I know I keep telling myself but then there's

danger in streetcars and the sadness in jays fans
and drake ALL OURS I mean CITY PRIDE I mean

at least two future cop choppers now low concussive
spotlights in shit bucket clouds A magic bullet sky

hard-selling the obstacle of downtown Why
more than one? The Church Fans Of The System

sounds like dumb panic but really this is
panicking The shadows off grace real good hiding

but just for a while The ash bark gone full spread
with ice water eyes Black squirrels sparkling

like warm steak knives for my twix bars This is our
City Within A Park's whole dog bowl grove marked

with an X. So bright with a good plan for death.
Wheezy stardust sucking on gold cellophane

where they buried the garrison in a gravel pit.
And we are all friends till the snacks run out.

Care enough about either of us. She will indulge herself a little. Telling it again this way: she grew till 17 and a half. A madness, she insists, she kept up at her mother's behest. How my grandmother, a woman all of 4'8"—her size-five shoes handed down to me till I was ten—desperately, desperately wanted her hunching daughter to make it to at least five feet. How *budvig* and two cups of powdered milk every day would ensure it. As tall a daughter as she could get. How my grandmother, who cut my mother's hair a twee bowl till she was 12 to thicken it past the thickness of her own childishly genteel locks—hair I never quite failed to call *cheveux d'ange*, like the pasta, picking at her bi-yearly perm while she cackled[9]—would have done everything in her power to will my wee mother's bones up. How she prayed. And my mother answered. By standing exactly five feet. Much taller than she should have been. And stopped drinking milk for a decade.

My mother's hair, forever since, is so thick. She hunches to this day.

9 My grandmother, the kind to make minimum payments on a couch for 12 years while the full amount, twice over, sat in the bank. Never lived in a house with showers, only baths. Raised two children in a tiny, paper-walled one-bedroom apartment.

And couldn't find a reason good enough to leave it, even after decades. Until the exterminator living in the basement experimented with roaches.

Kept her cheating, cheap, abusive husband around just the same. Until I was five. Only stopped wearing the ring when her finger got too fat.

And let me at it when her hair had fully flattened out. Would hand over her old boar bristle brush. The gross one now poking out of her old silver cup. Warming my desk. In the morning sun.

The kind to always think of whatever her housecleaning clients handed down as nothing less than generous thanks.

Always took pride in the lawyer- and doctor-gifted sideboard, claw-foot armchair, repro Art Nouveau side table, and Art Deco crystal stemware.

Never thought of our old barrister's bookcase—M. Stein #9 scrawled indelibly on the top third of the back—as anything else than hard evidence of respect.

Even as she more than doubled her forty-years-in-the-business, six-days-a-week income when, at 65, she retired on the minimum pension.

And finally curbed her husband.

look a lot like winning on the tv

and becomes my prime time
    name and calling
at the break

styling me the man's wee star
    searching patent
two face and trick

and his ain't ever quiet
    his insoluble little yap
congenital little skid

his zygotic lip and smacking
calls me scuzzlebutt
    his dopplered snort

and stalk
    his not quite
unoriginal mark made

calls me my father's son
    and no other word
but I could kill him

young man
and I'm storming
    the whole den

calls me mouth
    I better recognize
his could snap like a twig

reminds my arm like one
first time I make a fist
and the man stops laughing

the one chip off the old block
mr eyeball to eyeball
and his gene for an ass whooping

fights my gene for restraint

The kind of man who talks every other man on the street into building our deck. Printed every college paper in navy blue ink. Slurped—I'd clench my jaw—like everything just then was his. His house. His table. His son. And couldn't help but try to talk every stranger in The Body Shop into at least really liking him. Almost always the one Black man in the room. His singular twice as good as. His, our, golden ratio. Already always performing.

The kind of man to steal the bottle of bubbly at a staff dinner on a dare—everybody laughing. Mission accomplished. And to get fired in the morning. Liked drinking. And didn't care to stop driving when he did. Which finally got my mother learning stick.

A man beloved, at least for a while, by everybody. But always the few good breaths away from showing himself. Fired more times than I want to recount. But so charming no one would believe either of us. The wispy mother and son.

Until they saw it. Him shrieking at us losing Little Leaguers the one time we lost. Every other little boy crying, shocked. Screaming in the movie theater about Fuzzy Peaches. Slamming the brakes on the highway again. Thwacking me around the back seat. Rattling the door off its hinges. Always ready. To win the argument. His hand around the nape of my neck. His mouth inching toward my face. Always something about respect. Always to be repeated. On principle. And back to him. What I said. Never forget. Just what I said. Like you mean it. One more time. Again.[10]

10 The things he never failed to declare cultural. Which I couldn't help but be taught.

The things I learned to switch on. And had to. The years it took to switch them off.

Not qualified to raise a Black child on her own, his mother said. Can't divorce him, she said. And refused to talk to her at the service.

And would stare blankly at Bernard Shaw on CNN. That ain't a Black man, she'd say. Seemingly deaf to the sound of the son left to the care of the state.

You can walk like a nigga all you want, he'd say, but you ain't talking like one. What if his son became another nigger that doesn't trust him?

When the call came, it came in her voice, 11 years removed, thinking we were speaking again. Needing me to release the body. And donate it to the state.

Convinced the only thing between us was finally out the way.

One day, she's going to read this. Somehow. I just know she will. And we may have already spoken for the last time.

Sweatshirt

That cool   squashing

second
crawl space   His
smell   Cuts   open

Clapping back   the   lure
and   turn
around the hem Scraping
like a turtle

catches   a
light   long way
Getting   good

Barns Are Painted Red Because of the Physics of Dying Stars

I keep staring the notes gotta
mean something in a minute

Temporal doily   Doggerel on the lake
    Make a day of a wool habit

Now the Tate leads to the
NY library leads to Spitzweg
Beltracchi   Wisakedjak
to muskrat to grey jay
      Pitt shirtless in Fury

   Becomes no shame in sequence
Clear your history anyways

Stay Focusd   Bishop sequins
   Ship Hitachi to girlfriend
Say rue full   not rue flay

And do your to-do list   Eat this chicken
    like a chicken mechanic
        Make your mouth a wrench

Note desire for more cows is
the smart translation of war
    in Sanskrit   I love that

        I've missed being wanted

Her mouth sweetly on
about grool and the sheets

and two puppies and a sausage link

Softly *56 nucleons*
Softly *We're out of milk*

Get eggs while you're at it
gently pets me out of bed

. . . .

To think
we've each managed
season-long flits

our bones
light as feathers
the illusion
of each other's pelt

. . . .

Now it's hard
to enliven any of it

startled by your hand

. . . . . .

Now you hold my foot
with your ice-pack toes

like you mean it
somewhere else

. . . . .

How neither of us
wish to rewrite or relive
or can
quite yet

. . . .

You
polishing haikus
about polishing

Me
unearthing Stevens
    desperate
for the both of us

. . .

Now whispering his vagaries
for you under the covers

every tidy confusion

. .

How my sotto breaks
To touch a woman
            cadaverous

Your hand wet
from yourself

.

How we try
what we have

Spoon

The snow plow into the police car
into the bus into the truck
that hit the other bus
that hit everything else
gone viral

Not different but
now to me shrunken as if
on a long-standing whim
to remain very hidden
to be entered
via a hairline fracture

in everything he returned to
his whole life That shrine
still swelling marianne
slushy as of monday

The room still baby voice
with wittle cutie spoon
or be spooned mouthed
in her moonshine hallelujah

We ain't going anywhere
this weekend she tells

until we make it
back from riverdale
amen

Get that pizza
in the oven

Two hours into the three-hour argument about the pimento cream cheese and 12-grain sandwich, an interesting fact. The linen closet's wide-open corner just outside my second-floor boyhood bedroom retains just enough of a sightline down past the upper staircase, over the jumbo soft maple dining room table he badly wanted (the one end then a few months cratered by a wedding plate he had smashed on it), and between the long end of the L-shaped counter and the overhead kitchen cabinets, that the half-eaten sandwich just barely managed to bellyflop the sink's dirty dishwater when I whipped it. And it splashed him.

The sandwich's salmon-egg pink smeared into the side of my nine-year-old face while he screamed *EAT IT*. And I wondered if what was happening counted as physically abusive, and if I had any immediate regrets. The interesting fact being: somehow I didn't think so. Somewhere my mother was out making sure we got fed, weekly clippings in hand. All over basic cable, cartoons were proceeding without my attention, indifferent. I don't think I said anything when she got in. [11]

11 My father's last-ever room, in my godparents' basement in Hatboro, PA, is smaller than his old office, my teenage room, in my mother's basement. A Red Sox All-Star jersey hangs off an exposed pipe headed to the septic tank. The ensuite bathroom is Marines-themed—courtesy of his basement roommate—down to the towels and shower curtain. His tattered *Paradise Lost* still an eye-roll on the nightstand.

The sound of the roommate, meanwhile, on the other side of the wall. Cleaning a couple of clinking handguns.

Before bedtime, he shows me his mini-fridge stash of Klondike bars. My mother, conked out from the drive, already asleep upstairs. *Blazing Saddles* on TBS.

One way to think of
my father's mother is
she made what we got.

1. Routinely lined up
a cotton-hot iron to heat
the bedroom doorknob,

2. locking him on
the other side when
she needed a break.

3. The secured iron
slowly rendering the knob
unsafe, my father

4. banging on the door
as she walked out
of the apartment.

Or just beat him.
Sometimes with the iron.
I saw the scars.

Fruit of the ocean month. Fight about the library. Feculents. Closing soon. Asking about the computer. Ecreamed milk. Explosion. Fight about seeing each other. Herring, mackerel, and salmon. Only thirty minutes. Fight about language. Sardines and melon. Fight about badminton. Dill shrimp. David not understanding the thing about badminton. Fight about the garbage. The bed of rice, low-fat feta, cantaloupe wedges. *Chicane* (fight) about chocolate. Spicy French toast. The school's funding drive. Let rest. Fight about *Liar, Liar.* Grams of fat. At Video Plus. Fight in front of Eaton's. Grease holder, parcoured distance. About her not wanting to wait 45 minutes until it opens. A little extra. Fight about David's homework. Pie plate. David's sleeping bag. Thick tranches. About David asking how to save a file. Blank tuna. About his school bag, vegetables, etc. Zest, vanilla and *muscade.* Night fights about his apple (heart). Broccoli *quiche sans pâte.* About yelling. Little bouquets. Fights about mentioning there's snow again. The night before. And about snow on the ground, surprise, in the morning. A fine paste. Fight about the gas. Margarine. Fight about parquet for the office. A half-moon of Boston. And cheapness. Fight about blaming. Real parmesan cheese. David and language. Three-herb. All our problems. The walking away. The folding. Fight about the chicken again.[12]

12 About a year removed from him, sunk into the decades-old, formless sofa, in front of *Dawson's Creek* with my mother, outcast but by design, I tell her what it is and I beg for meds.

I tell her there's nothing else I can do right now. Just TV and French YA crap. She can't imagine it won't pass.

A few of the many things
she denies ever doing,
has claimed no memory of,
before he was taken away.

And before she refused to take
him back. Before the white
in his voice came in.

Before she helped raise
a partner's son. Her own
with the Salvation Army.

Before it became a story
he'd tell just about anyone,
but never his only child.

13

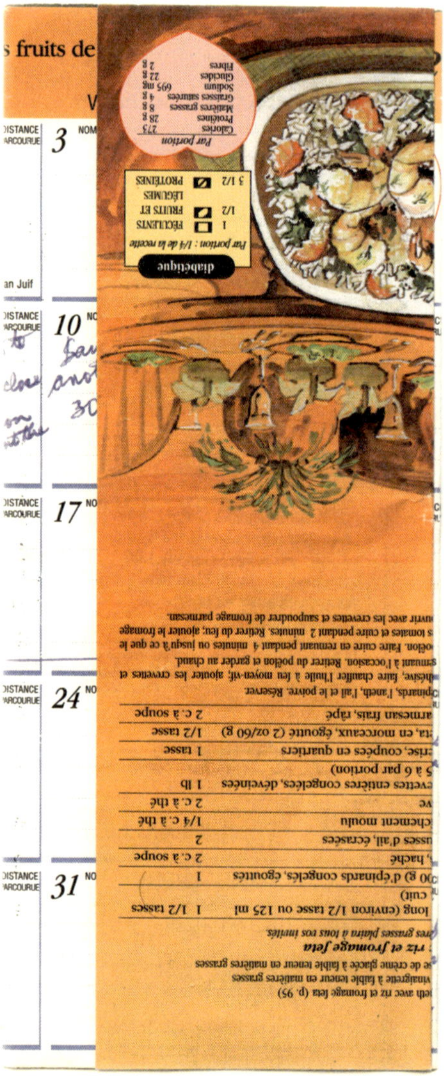

13 Because, 17 years in, it still didn't quite seem to my mother she had done all she could. She took notes. Four weeks of arguments. On a "seafood month" calendar from the office.

Spilling out of the square, or rerouting to the weekly "fat counter" box, on six separate occasions.

Both of them took to hiding
from the rest of us.

In his office every Christmas Eve.
Celebrating the holidays with PBS.

Her already always wheezing.
The same what would
kill him in a couple of decades.

Me always sneaking in. Just
to feel I could. Even feeling
what was on its way again.
Boiling over every year.

Why are you so *angry*,
she'd start in. Like
it was a given there was
no good answer he could offer.

Slurped
everything just
stranger in the Body

kind of bubbly

in the morning

A beloved
few breaths
to recount
wispy

lost little
highway
Rattling
around
my neck
Always
back
One more time

or if it comes to me
just the right titled
Just Cause

Lost Causes
Find the Junkyard Kindles
Raisc the Sand
and they will come

calling it Audible Sage Brush in the Wind
Run On Mouth Open
hot for New Ideas on Shining
and they will come

ride out The Beast Pastoral
Hometown Canvasser's Song
One Way Bridge Alight Out of Town
and they will come

for The Most Adult
Life Liquidation Sale
This Way the Scenic Routes
Out to Nowheres

All That Will

come as Springtime in Departures
and Power as Vegetarianism
Nature's Lifers at Fort Kindness
and they will come

for The Dear Let Go Love
Of the Refuge of the Department

suckers for The Wee Lossless Build
The Aaaaarg Buffet

for The Visceral Realism of Funions
Stone Soupier Saloners
Shtickless and Full Triscuit
and they will come

for Whatever Happens Now
That New Life for Communion
is Missing the Latest Wave
for Day-Old Donuts and Friends

'Cause They Will

all Plum Sweet as Hunters
On Good Will Less Sausage
More Freedom Forever Home
for Auntie Men

come the Good Lord's
Hoodrat Antiquarians
The Kid Leather of All In Statements
to Protect Us While They Last

And They Will

come in White Knuckle Prayers
Ready to Tear Shit Up
Just About Out of Here
If Nothing Changes

A Way Way On

Dance for New Answers
come The Rhetoric of Asking
Out in the Elliptical Open

A New Roof on the House
Of Lifelong Crying
Raised on Active Listening
For Active Listeners

Slubby Hearts Breathing in the Circle

come to Talk Out This Burning
Light the Found Road Again
Some Actual Together at a Reading
All that Building

Come None Too Late
for No Holding In
This Group Doc We're Starting
We the Campfire Kids

The Pain Angels Eat
Loud and Bright Again
And They're Coming
Just Not All of Them

Exactly

enough of
this
behest
handed down

ever a
cut twee
a thickness
a never quite *d'ange*
picking at while
to will my
bones my
exactly should be

My ever so thick [14]

14 Or too far.

Always asking her whose child I was. As she combed over the flyers by the checkout. Her visible, active worship of coupons. The way she licked her thumb. The potential nowhere we were headed. The one she was saving us from. Before moving on to the next one. Budgeting. On her own. Against my father. Wanting everything. Who would be heard wanting it. Against the way he called her cheap. And called the house a starter unit. Even as she struggled to pay for it. On her own. Against the ways his return to work meant his insistence on tassel loafers. Glenmorangie and steak lunches. Gabardine. A good pleat. His collars needing a better starching. Against a push that never stopped. Even suffocating. Even on her own. Dragging me on to the next bargain bins every other weekend. Even amidst the many, many shopkeepers and their unabashed marvelling. Such a loaf-golden boy. Such a freckled, hook-nosed white woman. *Whose* I was. No matter what. Her very own.[15]

15 Decades later, she tells me at an early breaking point in those last few years, the two of them came to agree—something might be wrong with him. His complete ups and downs. And he sought real help. His case deemed a serious one. Escalated to a province-appointed psychiatrist. In a matter of months. Unheard of.

Only to be discarded as a bully in the first session. The white doctor refusing to even attempt to put any other word on what he had going on. Didn't reassign him to anyone else. Just turned him out. No answers at all.

16

16 His every objection: pasted in throughout returned copies of her emails; enlarged and *italicized*; and appearing in *ALL CAPS*, ***bolded***, and/or <u>under-lined</u> wherever he deemed appropriate. As if to will an ongoing argument. Off and on for years.

What I know is he left it up to me. Asking me to need him. I think. Or at least to want to say I need him. Incant change. A different, real or better, father-and-son thing. Something neither of us *got*. Neither of us had ever been. A job waiting for him in Connecticut. Only if I okayed it.[17]

He asked like he knew something. Something mutual now. And not knowing how I'd spent the last two years. Trying to convince her to get rid of him. Taking note after note of the mess, him laying it out, watching him. Making use of his not-taking-no-for-an-answer thing. Watching her clean it up. Over and over again.

My point to her, those years, was: if you keep having to clean it up then you ain't cleaning shit; aren't you tired yet? I was, and I watched her refuse to give in to it. Listen and try again. Thinking he'd get better after school. Paying into it. Or in a job he likes. Waiting him out. And again. Until even she saw no other option but to end it.[18]

What I saw, meanwhile, was what I might become one day. An angry man who can't do anything without someone else paying for it. How ugly it might look. And suddenly a chance. To never see any of it again. To shrug and let him know I don't give a shit. Not ever again. Knowing what I might seal in. And out. With one last argument.[19]

How he would cease to be a resident. Not in this country. And would have to ask permission. Even just to visit. And she'd let me give it as little as I wanted.

And I got what I wanted.[20]

17 Would he feel abandoned? Or relieved? At first? The first in a long line of layoffs. The shock of what would pass for benefits.

18 The no citizenship, the citizenship he'd scoffed at, he'd come to regret.

19 The twenty years it would take me to make it to what might be mine to regret.

20 The less than two years it took him to go bankrupt. Even with his borrowing against our life insurance. Money she saw to it we got back.

«Les yeux dans graisse de bines»

lest my very own grecian hew

    dawn the graze
of the densest bines

or when my yew graced dances
    my lesser beens behind

packs it in for the night

the way she places both
    dans le même trou

her eyes in the same hole

and points out mine
    bothered with every stare

are like his were

    ailing with every yawn

baneful as the man's crow's
    feet grousing the corners out

tu bailles aux corneilles   she sighs

    clicking both bedside lights off

the motel clicker still flickering
    thru the sports channels

Decades later, she tells me she was already ready to end it that very first college year.

What followed instead was another eight years of marriage. Worsening migraines. Sciatica. The early onset of osteoporosis. The long, ebbing feeling of failure. An argument calendar, for safe measure. Settling the divorce with her first-ever brand-new car.

Then the iron-willed year of suburban buses, the next three years to pay off a new burgundy Corolla, the other five it took her for the house. Eight years of the first boyfriend and his dumb sweetness and kindness and his dead daddy issues catalyzed into a deep, addicted love—how happy she was. My departure. His eventual gambling problem. All his mother's savings gone. Only a few grand of my mother's. Paid off with the Corolla.

Every one of those years she saved compulsively. Whatever she could. And suddenly found herself, as she put it, sitting on more money than she could possibly bring herself to spend. Almost ashamed of it. And meaning to share it. Long before she dies.[21]

21 My lounging mother in her favourite bunny pyjamas. Meaning for me to take advantage of the money, she said, before she dies.

That summer, I was able to quit one of my jobs. And had started writing again by Christmas.

But not a dime given and spent I haven't replaced. As if to pay for it. Small-cap dividends. Or warrant it. Checking the account. Tax-free. Accounts. Checking them again. Bearish sentiment. What could be gone. Trailing 12-month. That I may have cost anything at all. Monthly donation. Never quite not a problem.

Wipe

to read cat person
or just lie here

coffee's rocky cane
sugar down my chin

canola under the sole
tree in a big field

like a roof meant to soak
thru its all moving

limbs a cinema verily
a crispy happening

two piece before the rain
I eat very slowly

tender clucking as it
shrinks honey dripping

lines one bite at a time
run over my thigh bones

brimming as a birdbath

dawn and in droplets too : our hosiery and the horse face
our bestilledness and cut grease : up on all of it and yet

my order for trail shoes : our ascent around the apartment
our thundercat for the markets : in a pinch into the terrain

looky a tiny painter painted in big paints : old back to bed
a scroll tho very brightly : a little pose for the canyon's edge

just like that : a walk but dirty : the sponge in the microwave
the doorknob regimen again : think all the limbs out of frame

and many more : heading out now : and still with every trace
next episode : the latest package : another big protein shake

the five minutes before the washing away : our last dance
mr blackhead : not tired at all : the tea that never gets made

and on as if crackling

tiny panes off the little school
too cold in the wind chill

too flirted off a snap

a mid-century ending

glowing tuft of glass

pecks away all neck
right above my camera

all toes off the ground

all noonday foil and sun

a white light boring
in and out the branch

that will not break

that repeats itself

in thc finest sparking
knot nothing at all but *h ere!*

ere *h ere!* sapping up

a look down at no one

it hasn't seen before

How I know what he might have done in comparison.

How I shut my wee uncle the fuck down. His recounting an adult-sized Christmas dinner I was force-fed. I have no memory of. Over lunch with my girlfriend.

How my palm through the hall's pink wall. Meant her tiny fists into my chest. The man she was seeing again, 15 and crying.

What a dumb motherfucker thought, out to shout me down. To pay for the slice a second time. My father's voice clicking on. In my mouth. Shrivelling the little racist. Just like that.

What things a partner would yell. Desperate for any rise. What she couldn't get. *SHUT THE*—what I kept keeping in.

And how my fist, one last time. Went through the basement door. What a long time ago. When her first boyfriend said, *What would your father think*. What got me leaving. For her sake.

How well I could plan for the symptoms of him. What little I understood of them.

What remains in remove.

Dust off what movement. I can only hear.

A blue T-shirt out the giveaway pile I'm still walking around in.[22]

22 Russell Athletics, faded navy, a single dab of primer on the right sleeve. Still a perfect fit.

Another scrap I couldn't leave behind: two pages for Advanced Comp., tucked away in a briefcase stuffed with old chargers, about his childhood. Blaming himself for being taken away. And for telling his teachers he wasn't getting fed at home.

The other men. At least a little like him. Tying the deaf Dalmatian to the doghouse year round. Set to leave the country after borrowing money from the wrong people. Throwing the TV in the pool—she wouldn't hand over the remote. Casing and clipping bullets in the basement while we wait for the pizza. Just the ones on our street his age. Who built our deck on a whim.

Brought nail guns. Helped pick up the lumber. The one happy to foreman. The other, the one who'd leave, happy to draft. My father handled his father's mail for years after he left. Visited the old man every other week. Just because. Followed the other to softball. Had beers for weeks with TV after his daughter passed.

My father, who never forgot an aunt or uncle's name. Never had any of his own. And always made a point of saying hi, joking, laughing. Believed in family, even not knowing it. Never without a smile or googly eyes or compliment. For anyone else's kid. Wanting to be wanted. So badly. Always convincing that way.

Like how he wouldn't quit Little League till a few years after I did. And I resented it. His feeling useful. In a way he wouldn't at home. Another kind of ease out in the open.

Like, just recently, the man I'm barely remembering. Father and nice. I'm realizing he was from the year I was away. And I was just a kid to impress on weekends. How much easier it must have been for him. Just get the kid to like me. Extracurricular. Not yet granted. Rolling around in the leaves. Have his mother to myself all week. Snowball fights with the neighbour kids. Things those other men never did.

Like the night he died. At my godparents'. Talking to an old friend on the anniversary of his best friend's death. How this old friend happened upon him in little pieces in the jungle in Vietnam. And hasn't rung in a February 15th since without a bottle in hand. My father, that night, kept him laughing in the living room, away from drinking, past midnight. And made sure he made it to bed that way.

My father, just back from a business trip. Lungs still crackling from the thin Utah air. My godmother was the one who found him. Around four in the morning. In the bathroom. Lights on. Still standing.

He got so thin, she says. Just like me.[23]

23 Half of those other men are also dead now. The deck only a few years gone.

It occurred to me only recently. That the iron and doorknob trick may have been designed to protect him,

every time his mother did it, from her. That it was meant to keep her out of the room, not just him in.

There she was at the Human Gift Registry memorial in her best Candomblé whites,

in a wheelchair, surrounded by her chosen family and friends,

handing me a velvet pouch with a gold drawstring,

and I tried to think: maybe she actually doesn't remember any of it.

the ocean Closing
the Ecreamed
see n

thing about
garbage The bed of at

rest

Da Pie Da sleeping tranches

sans

the ground A fine
gas parquet

language
folding again

Or maybe what she took
up in herself then—a thing

at one time acted out on her,
then acted out on him—
was also happening to her.

The way the injured
get a mind to injure.

What was happening not just
to me but to my father.
Not just to my mother. Never

to be negotiated out loud.

Not that I know
what to do with that.

But I keep thinking on it.

and I liked it

everything now is
language : fat deli
pickle jars : cot myrtle
    and bog : hot
moonbeam in the mouth

compost speckling off
a last sputtering minute : down
out a ripped up puff jacket :
tickling the larynx : feathers
and sparkling : a quiet : is
    finally garbage : ready
                    to fly away

welcome to the dark side
    energy good
you can eat with my face

says clothes is nothing more than filling
a god-sized hole in all of us little ones

queenie as my dove my peal and diamonds

in your baby tux all you drag up and hold
with all your haring heart bares me straight

up in your pumps and naught but your long

palm our spitting image our pooling buff

how do you like that? Let it freckle and

hum free and round lashed good as I hear
the sashay out your nightgown my mouth

a puddle off your back so full as it whittles

your eyes so pretty out of focus your legs
so jelly-roll my neck out of orbit tuck and say

the word lead on I will follow with my lips

Attention

at the stove my being alive is
to never touch a star
again like it's nothing

said again nothing
enough it breaks
the indelicate bottom

open of my porcelain
baby owl mid lash
batting worry and glaze

over my stale jack pine
branch snappings up
the crackling lampshade

a shadow brocade itself
a nothing of mine
I notice to break

as the neighbour's boy
takes his teething stick
out his doggy face

and begins to articulate
three long stories
below the pigeon shit

pink contrapuntal of brick
a big silent message
I watch off his lips

understanding nothing

at all but my focus
off the kitchen ledge

not breaking the window
that seals the kettle
that screams the dog

who waves

And I can't unthink it.

The last two remaining Bradfords.

The abused son of the abused father

reaching out to the survivor-survivor
grandmother, the still-hanging-on-
by-the-oxygen-tank daughter
of a brothel's madam.

Everything to wade thru forever
trickling in the muddied background.

Everything else gone.

I think of calling her. I don't.

I can't remember what color
the pouch was because
I left it in Philadelphia.

About a month away from Medicare, which would have afforded him his oxygen tank. Suddenly nothing left for me to protect against. And a sudden opening. A kind of compassion, and preordained bad timing. Neither of which got me closer to crying.

Then, over an early dinner one late afternoon that spring, I cued up *He Got Game*. I sat down to a two-piece of fried chicken—a little treat after a good day of writing. The camera wafted over Middle America on its way into the city, montaging, basketballs and young men's hands—solo and mid-game, slow-motion air play—Kansas, Indiana, the Northwest seaside, Staten Island. Copland's "John Henry" ("A Railroad Ballad for Orchestra") weaving every gesture and pasture into a single, dancing opening. And no more than 15 seconds in, it started. Denzel's Jake Shuttlesworth brow and gaze in the noonday hoosegow sun. Ray Allen's Jesus Shuttlesworth, the son, and his pure shot spliced in. My mouth splayed so wide open chicken was falling out of it.

Three years later, it still works if I need it to. Something still new I'm trying to live without.[24]

24 The last place I saw or spoke to my father was a 12th-floor room at the Days Inn by the Trudeau Airport nine years ago. My jaw still clenching from the drive back from Burlington. His hug and demand that I call him. *I love you, Son.* My secret resolve. To never see him again.

And I couldn't bring myself to say it back.

Could I say it now, if I could bring myself back to it? Would I say *Dad*?

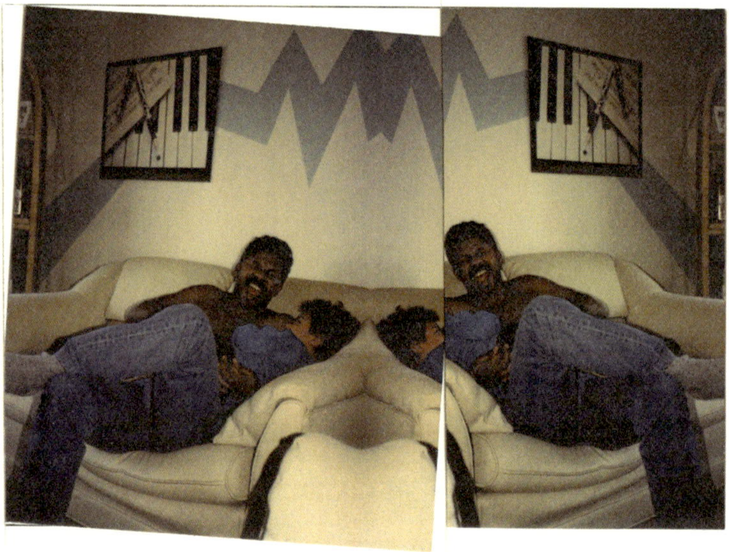

Now I smell like him.

His bed-head, his bad breath,
his sweat. His mother's
pretty eyebrows on my face.

His eyes, part, and
sloping, crooked hairline. His
scrawling, cursive hand.

Barely anything at all.
None of it going away.

When I pulled the pouch's
drawstring, I found a small
account closure cheque

and his oversized, empty wallet.

The creditors got everything else.

Pitch

I'd like to like this blue bathtub
The echo in it   rung tired
    of my filth

        Is the conjugate animal
the gallop   that the mandible
  can't hold or break

    Even to wade
out blue in the mend   crack
    blown out a silver shade

marbling up the water   troubled
    three alarm riser
  bubbled in a bellied heat

          whole empty
of what blue fish may miss
  the sea   I wish

    waiting out this slow
  slow week   clearly in August
    abuzz with bluebells

could blow the house
    a few small feet east
  into a different breeze

    I just need
      to keep changing
one more thing that can't

firm belabouring
tells me in gossip

scapegoating is by tradition
natural as lisping
to Galician

is thick   forever culture
never discussed
as impending

Says the present just is
always there again
repeating itself

like it's haunting   imposed
as a gift   a hearing
in every quiet ending

pretending agreement
The bar is ankle low
for all these people

behaving   Insists
the best salad in here
is the banquet

burger   laid out on kale
dressing on the side
with tempeh bacon

They are still okay
outlawing our good frolic

Ain't no dead end

anything you can't call
a bridge   Remember
who's to be cheated

she says   early
and often   laughing
then has me fed

Little miracle but

that much more   concise is
my ass   atop low-top sneakers

This all I’ve got
is my human look   to be
known by   too little   too much
    thought to handhold a gaze

my commuter legs   up
    to my voice box in meaning
        to be   looked at
while my mouth is open

What can be done of watching
        for being watched is
    I worry   about all of it

and lose things

This purposeful hind of me
gone easy   those few years
    I walked a camera instead

        before I found it again

    a poem

        I don’t deservèd

[soft-shoeing across marble

[cooling perfect sale fruit
cobbler

Where did I take that?

All day off on missing parts
and not getting shortlisted

hungry for ice cream
These fucking kids

doing my back exercises
are killing No one

What was the Nowhere?

Can I Shut up

I just Up

Keep Breathing

after Sonia Sanchez

Given not so much
    an artefact A debris
        kind of field

Given the moaning
    come out ain't ever
        the problem

Given you get as far
    as the ceiling You sit
        long and hard enough

given it move your big teeth
        out your work arm
    off your throat

    out the give you cut
thru your good people
        Your buck mouth

up to Fuck Yourself
        Gives light a mirror
    out your bloat chest

kissed so clean up out
    the room   wings so shed
        of your bullshit

    it give in the sweetest
        you ever been on a bearing
Claps in Fuck Your Mess

Up a hot mass
out your head
It keeps you breathing

And you keep breathing
the end

What left Asking
a different
o ther us

a mutual
last Try
rid of

a clean and over

a tired
fail to give get better after
Or out

what might be
d one for it

might

cease to be
just
as little as

wanted

On the phone, I finally ask my mother about her own mother's death. *The absence, you know, doesn't go away,* she says. Always something you need you're still learning to not need. She wishes I'd known her as a younger woman—how full of energy she could be, a big, tiny woman on a table leading songs at wedding parties. How she had a thing for men on motorcycles way back in the townships.

But also, she starts telling me about her father's long, filed fingernails, how he was the one to teach her how to write, which made it easier for her to go into first grade early at five. How her mother worked so much he was, in an odd way, the more present but absent one. How, unusually, for the time, he was into tanning. Burned his uniform when he came back from deployment—a dramatic man. And took them to Parc Belmont on Saturdays. Taught them to draw, homebound as he was during those early depressions, which explains more than I wish it did about my uncle.

In my stuffy, carpeted bedroom, I take her off speakerphone and she reveals that my grandfather, a few winters before he died, almost tried to kill himself on the edge of the Saint-Laurent. He told my uncle. He couldn't go on without women. She tells me he was the kind of man who needed to fuck—on the phone, she says *make love*, which is worse—four times a day until he couldn't at all. I'd heard it before, but it sinks in this time. That his mother, back in New Brunswick, would hide from company like a cat, anxiety and depression too deep in the bloodline. But also, that most of the women she knows her age had horrible, distant, war-torn fathers. And she gets it. But they never forgave him how he treated their mother. And learned to hate him for it.

It always astounded her that, at times, even amidst it all, they were so in love. Her mother so devastated when she realized he really wouldn't stop seeing other women. There was likely a woman, or women, she surmises, in Florida. But her mother was so in love. And so loyal. But what she misses the most now that she's gone is just talking to her. She was always such a good ear. Always a crier. Which is where she starts crying. She was doing a crossword when I called.

I want to tell her I'm here for her, but she beats me to it. *I've always been able to talk to you*, she says, something that's come easily. And continues to. Although, she did worry about burdening me when I was younger. *Stuff too heavy for a 16-year-old*, she says. No idea what she's referring to. Which I guess is the point. Before parting, she wonders when I might visit again.[25]

After we hang up, I watch a couple of hours of *Voyager*, prepare for a reading, stretch my back and go to bed. I think about sleeping in my father's basement bed. The *semper fi* paraphernalia in the bathroom. *Blazing Saddles* blaring through the door. Finally learning the fat end of an earplug is best the first to go in. On the other side of my bedroom wall, Gino, the landlord, coughs like he's dying. I sleep poorly as usual. Dream of no one but myself.

25 Unsure when I might say I'll make it back, I ask her what she's been reading instead.

Actually, novels, she says. Whodunits, her mother's Poirots, that kind of stuff. And enjoying it. I can hear her smiling on the line.

I tell her I'll look for a train in the morning. I book a ticket in the middle of the night.

now might have done

my wee own count
fed no

How my palm fi ts
n a

What a thought
second voice clicking In
Just

What rise
kept keeping

said *What would*
me a n

well the little

remains

I'm still walking in

Cute Bear

Rock darned
        to singsong
the elements

        out my pocket
    the ghosts too many
            in the quiet

too quick before
    our bedtime   followed
        by robots of the night

This is your prone breath
    in the first heat wave
            so sticky

    with no touching I'm
obbligato and   chill
    cute bear mauling

cottage piano   Esther Perel
        real live couple's therapist
    charming a hole in my hand

Stroke sheet blotto
to that deep *I'll never be safe*
    here just existing   I hate

my dad was right
    place   and sorry
for your face right then

Your thumb on my lip
so done with me
for the night

and sweet as salt fish

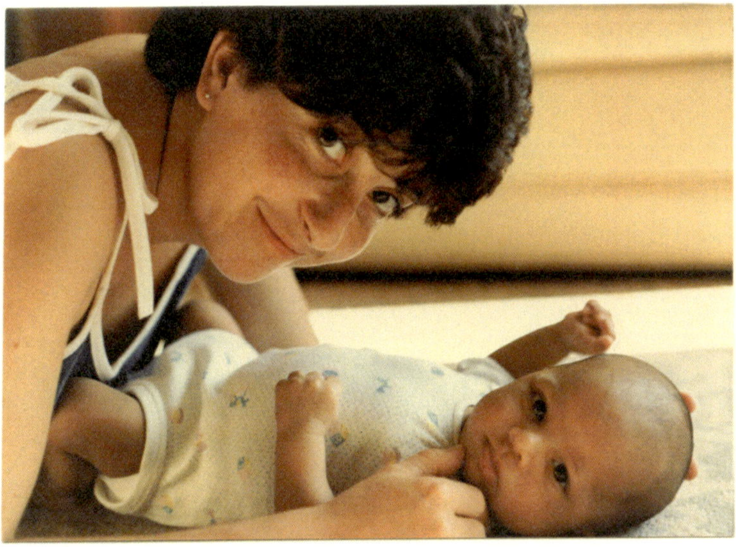

Notes

All of the pictures repurposed for this book are my family pictures, used with my mother's permission.

All of the writings defaced for the visual poems that accompany "The Plot" are my own.

The Dawn Lundy Martin epigraph is taken from *Good Stock Strange Blood.*

The Renee Gladman epigraph is from *Calamities.*

21: The footnote to "The Shower" makes reference to Christakos's *Her Paraphernalia: On Motherlines, Sex, Blood, Loss & Selfies.*

55: The title "Barns Are Painted Red Because of the Physics of Dying Stars" is taken from an article of the same name from the Smithsonian Magazine website, as is the phrase "56 nucleons."

The phrase "desire for more cows" is taken from the film *Arrival* (2016).

58: The unforgettable problem of a phrase "to touch a woman cadaverous" is from "Arcades of Philadelphia the Past" by Wallace Stevens.

67: "Refuge of the department" I owe to Fred Moten and Stephano Harney's *The Undercommons.*

"Lifelong Crying" I owe to Arthur Symons's "The Crying of Water," via W.E.B. Du Bois's *The Souls of Black Folk.*

"The Pain Angels Eat" I owe to Nathaniel Mackey's "Song of Andoumboulou: 9."

78: "a tiny painter in big paints" refers to Dorothea Tanning's *Self Portrait* (1944).

87: "The Sun Set / and I liked it" is taken from the song "Sun's Rays (Energy Good)" by Bog Myrtle.

88: "god-sized hole" I owe to RuPaul speaking to Oprah (2018).

Acknowledgments

Earlier forms of some of the poems in this book found their way into a number of journals. To the editors and readers at *Prairie Fire*, *Poetry Is Dead*, *Faded Out*, *The Trinity Review*, *The Unpublished City*, *The Capilano Review*, *Invisiblog*, *Vallum*, *filling Station*, and *the tiny*, thank you.

This book might not exist without Dionne Brand, and the pushes and permissions granted and needed.

This book might not exist without the support of Catherine Bush, who made it feasible for me to go all in when it was time.

This book also found many invaluable readers, boosters, and encouragers at various stages on its way here. Thanks to Hoa Nguyen and Erin Robinsong, my first readers. Thanks to Rose Cullis, Lindsay Miles, Jacquelyn Ross, the whole Guelph crew. Thanks to Alisha Kaplan, Lauren Turner, Cassidy McFadzean, Anahita Jamali Rad, Canisia Lubrin, Alex Leslie, Kevin Connelly, Michael Nardone, Leigh Nash, Andrea Actis, and River Guri. Thanks to Ralph Kolewe and Norm Nehmetallah. Thanks to Hilary Martin. Thanks to Kaie Kellough. Thanks to Emma Brown Sanders. Thanks to AJ Little. Thanks to jes dolan, for all the hype and all the smoke.

Thanks to my editor Sonnet L'Abbé, and for all those long back-and-forths.

Thanks to my partner Kara Sterne for all the talks, for all the readings when there was nothing much here, and then a bit more, and then a bit more.

Thanks to my godparents, always, for taking care of my father.

And thanks to my mother. For everything. For being so open to this. We're still here.

David Bradford is a poet, editor, and organizer based in Tiohtià:ke (Montréal). He holds an MFA from the University of Guelph. *Dream of No One but Myself* is his first book.